Mutual Funds

How To Make Saving and Investing Easier and Safer

MOODY PRESS
CHICAGO

© 1994 by
AUSTIN PRYOR

ISBN 0-8024-3991-8

Library of Congress Cataloging in Publication Data

1 3 5 7 9 10 8 6 4 2

Printed in the United States of America

FOREWORD

I have known Austin Pryor for almost twenty years now, and I regard him as a good friend. As I have observed him over the years, I have found his counsel to be both biblical and practical. I know of no other individual with whom I would consult with more confidence on the subject of mutual fund investing than Austin.

I believe the true character of an investment adviser is not only the degree of success he has achieved, but the integrity that is maintained in the process. Austin has achieved success in the business world, but, more important, he has done so with truth and honesty.

Obviously you, the reader, must evaluate his advice yourself. No one individual has the right advice for everyone, and anyone can, and will, be wrong in the changing economy we live in. But if you will spend the time to read carefully the counsel Austin provides, you will find it both time and money well spent.

I encouraged my good friends at Moody Press to contact Austin about publishing his writing because I felt he had information that would benefit God's people. We are in no way competitors. Austin and I are collaborators in God's plan to help His people become better stewards of His resources.

Larry Burkett

The biblical principles reflected in this booklet are the foundation for the advice given in *Sound Mind Investing*, my book published by Moody Press. The material in this booklet has, for the most part, been excerpted from that book. As Christians, we acknowledge God as the owner of all. We serve as His stewards with management privileges and responsibilities. The practical application of biblical principles leads us to encourage a debt-free lifestyle and conservative approach to investing such as that shown in what we call the Four Levels of Investing:

Level One: Getting Debt-Free
"The rich rules over the poor, and the borrower becomes the lender's slave."
Proverbs 22:7

Paying off debts which are carrying 12%-18% per year interest charges is the best "investment" move you can make. So, get to work on paying off those credit cards, car loans, student loans, and other short-term debts. Accelerating the payments on your house mortgage, if any, should also be your goal—albeit a longer-term one. It should be your first priority to see the day when you're meeting all current living expenses, supporting the Lord's causes, and completely free of consumer debt.

Level Two: Saving for Future Needs
"There is precious treasure and oil in the dwelling of the wise, but a foolish man swallows it up." Proverbs 21:20

Even if you've not completely reached your Level One goal, it's still a good idea to set aside some money for emergencies or large purchases. A prudent rule of thumb is that your contingency fund should be equal to three to six months living expenses. We suggest $10,000 as an amount suitable for most family situations.

Level Three: Investing in Stocks
*"Well done, good and faithful servant. You were faithful with a few things,
I will put you in charge of many things." Matthew 25:21*

Only money you have saved over and above the funds set aside in Level 2 should be considered for investing in the stock market. In Levels One and Two, any monthly surplus was used in a manner that *guaranteed* you would advance financially—there are no guarantees in the stock market. You should initiate a program of mutual fund investing geared to your personal risk temperament and the amount of dollars you have available to invest.

Level Four: Diversifying for Safety
*"Divide your portion to seven, or even to eight, for you do not know what
misfortune may occur on the earth." Ecclesiastes 11:2*

Once you accumulate $25,000 in your investment account, it's time for further diversification. By adding investments to your holdings that "march to different drummers," you can create a more efficient, less volatile portfolio. The single most important diversification decision is deciding how much to invest in stocks versus bonds. That's why determining your personal investing temperament, and following the guidelines given, can be so helpful.

Free Upon Request

Articles that guide you through the Four Levels—help on getting debt-free, saving strategies, and updates on specific no-load mutual fund recommendations that are geared to your personal risk tolerance—appear in my monthly newsletter, also called *Sound Mind Investing*. In it, I offer a conservative investing strategy based on the careful use of no-load mutual funds. For a free sample copy, simply return the postage-paid card included at the back of this booklet.

What Mutual Funds Are and Their Advantages to Investors

I. **For most investors, mutual funds represent the best way to assemble a well-balanced, diversified portfolio of securities.**

A. A mutual fund is simply a big pool of money formed when thousands of small investors team up in order to gain advantages that are normally available only to wealthy investors.

B. When you add your money to the pool, you are given shares to show what portion of the pool belongs to you.

C. The money in the pool is managed by a hired professional who is paid based upon the size of the pool and, in some cases, on his/her performance results.

D. The money in the pool can only be invested according to the "ground rules" that were drawn up when the pool was first formed. Most mutual funds limit their investments to a particular kind of stock or bond.

II. Mutual funds can reduce the anxiety associated with investing due to their many advantages, which make your investing easier and safer.

A. They reduce risk by providing extensive diversification. This means their price movements are less volatile and more predictable than individual stocks.

B. They provide experienced, full-time professional management that gives your holdings individual attention on a daily basis.

C. Past performance is a matter of public record.

D. You can efficiently reinvest your dividends.

E. They offer many convenient services, such as automatic investing and withdrawal plans, check-writing privileges, handling all the paperwork, creating reports for tax purposes, and providing safekeeping of your money.

F. They can be used for your IRA and other retirement plans.

G. They allow you to sell your shares and leave the pool at any time.

The easiest way to understand a mutual fund is to think of it as a big pool of money.

The *Barron's Dictionary of Finance and Investment Terms* defines a mutual fund as a "fund operated by an investment company that raises money from shareholders and invests it in a variety of securities." My plain-English definition is that it's (1) a big pool of money (2) collected from lots of individual investors (3) that is managed by a full-time professional investment manager (4) who invests it according to specific guidelines. When you put money in a mutual fund, you are pooling your money with other investors in order to gain advantages that are normally available only to the wealthiest investors. You are transformed from a small investor into part-owner of a multimillion dollar *portfolio*, or group of diverse investments.

What do you get in return for your investment dollars? You receive *shares* that represent your ownership in part of the pool. The value of the shares is calculated anew at the end of every day the financial markets are open. Here's how it's done. First, you take the day's closing market value of all the investments in the fund's pool. To that number, you add the amount of uninvested cash on hand that isn't invested for the time being (most funds keep 3%-5% of their holdings in cash for day-to-day transactions). That gives you the up-to-the-minute value of all the pool's holdings. Next, you need to subtract any amounts the pool owes (such as management fees that are due to the portfolio manager but haven't yet been paid). This gives the net value of the assets in the pool. Finally, we divide the net value by the total shares in the pool to determine what each individual share is worth. This is called the *net asset value* per share and is the price at which all shares in the fund will be bought or sold for that day. It is also the number that is reported in the financial section of the newspaper the next morning.

What kinds of *securities* do mutual funds invest in? That depends on the ground rules...

...set up when the pool was first formed. Every mutual fund is free to make its own ground rules. The rules are explained in a booklet called the *prospectus* that every mutual fund must provide to investors—that is where you learn what types of securities the fund is allowed to invest in.

Mutual funds invest in just about every type of security around, including corporate, government, and tax-free bonds, federally backed mortgages, and the ever-popular money market instruments like bank CDs, commercial paper, and U.S. treasury bills.

For the average person, mutual funds are the very best way to assemble a well-balanced, diversified portfolio containing many different kinds of securities. (But in order to simplify things, I'll primarily use mutual funds that are stock-oriented when I'm explaining how funds work.)

HOW THE XYZ MUTUAL FUND
CALCULATES ITS DAILY CLOSING PRICE

List of Investments	Closing Price	Shares Owned	Market Value
Alcoa	$71.13	6,400	$455,232
Allied-Signal	29.88	8,900	265,932
American Express	25.63	9,700	248,611
A T & T	37.13	7,500	278,475
Bethlehem Steel	15.88	12,000	190,560
Boeing	48.88	3,000	146,640
Caterpillar	51.75	7,200	372,600
Chevron	73.88	4,400	325,072
Coca-Cola	57.25	3,800	217,550
Disney	116.00	2,200	255,200
DuPont	47.25	3,500	165,375
Eastman Kodak	42.38	9,100	385,658
Exxon	58.25	6,000	349,500
General Electric	77.25	4,600	355,350
General Motors	43.13	6,600	284,658
Goodyear	26.25	8,400	220,500
IBM	106.13	3,300	350,229
International Paper	70.63	2,900	204,827
McDonald's	35.00	9,500	332,500
Merck	118.88	4,000	475,520
Minnesota Mining	95.25	3,500	333,375
J.P. Morgan	55.00	7,700	423,500
Philip Morris	68.38	2,300	157,274
Proctor & Gamble	85.13	3,100	263,903
Sears	40.63	5,000	203,150
Texaco	64.50	8,600	554,700
Union Carbide	20.00	9,200	184,000
United Technology	46.88	6,800	318,784
Westinghouse	29.75	7,000	208,250
Woolworth	33.38	9,500	317,110

Market Value of Investments	$8,844,035
Plus: Cash on Hand	+265,321
Less: Expenses Payable	-6,744
Net Value of Pool Assets	$9,102,612
Divide By: Number of Shares	524,388
Net Asset Value Per Share of Fund XYZ	$17.36

A mutual fund usually limits its investments to a particular kind of security. For example, assume you want to invest only in quality American blue chip stocks that pay good dividends. As it turns out, there are a large number of mutual funds whose rules permit them to invest only in such stocks. No small company stocks, overseas stocks, stock options, long- or short-term bonds, precious metals, or anything else. By limiting their permissible investments, mutual funds allow you to pool your money together with that of thousands of other investors who wish to invest in similar securities.

Mutual funds are almost certain to play an important role in your financial future because they offer you so many advantages that will make your investing program easier and safer. Here are 20 major advantages.

Advantage #1: Mutual funds can reduce the anxiety of investing.

Most investors constantly live with a certain amount of anxiety and fear about their investments. This is usually because they feel they lack one or more of the following essentials: (1) market knowledge, (2) investing experience, (3) self-discipline, (4) a proven game plan, or (5) time. As a result, they often invest on impulse or emotion. The advantages offered by mutual funds can go a long way toward relieving the burdens associated with investing.

Advantage #2: Mutual fund shares can be purchased in such small amounts that it makes it easy to get started.

If you have been putting off starting your investing program because you don't know which stocks to invest in and you can't afford your own personal investment consultant to tell you, mutual funds will get you on your way.

It doesn't require large sums of money to invest in mutual funds. Most fund organizations have minimum amounts needed in order to initially open your account, set from $500 to $3,000. And if even $500 is too much, some fund organizations (such as 20th Century Investors and the Invesco Group) have no minimum account requirement *if* you'll agree to make regular monthly deposits to build your account.

Advantage #3: Mutual fund accounts can also be added to whenever you want—often or seldom— in small amounts.

After meeting the initial minimum (if any) to open your account, you can add just about any amount you want. To make your purchase work out evenly, they'll sell you fractional shares. For example, if you invest $100 in a fund selling at $7.42 a share, the fund organization will credit your account with 13.478 shares ($100 deposit divided by $7.42 per share = 13.478 shares).

Advantage #4: Mutual funds reduce risk through *diversification*.

Most stock funds hold as many as 200 stocks in their portfolios. They do this so that any loss caused by the unexpected collapse of a single stock will have a minimal effect on the pool as a whole. Without the availability of mutual funds, the investor with just $2,000 to invest would likely put it all in just one or two stocks (a very risky way to go). But by using a mutual fund, that same $2,000 can make the investor a part owner in a large, professionally managed portfolio that often includes hundreds of stocks.

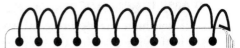

DIVERSIFICATION

means the spreading of investment risk by putting one's assets into many different kinds of investments.

Risk is usually defined in terms of the potential an investment has for wild swings up and down in its market value. The term "volatility" refers to the extent of these price swings. An investment with high volatility (meaning very wide, often abrupt, swings in its market value) is defined as high risk. An investment with low volatility (meaning narrow, usually gradual swings in its market value) is thought of as having low risk.

Mutual funds are usually regarded as relatively low in risk because they are so widely diversified. While some of their holdings are moving up in value, others are standing still or moving down. So, the price changes somewhat cancel each other out. The effect of this is to increase the price stability of the overall portfolio. Thus, while an investor is unlikely to score a huge gain in any one year holding mutual funds, he is also unlikely to incur a huge loss. This relative price stability is one of the primary advantages of investing through mutual funds for the average investor.

Advantage #5: Mutual funds' price movements are more predictable than those of individual stocks.

Their extensive diversification, coupled with outstanding stock selection, makes it highly unlikely that the overall market will move up without carrying almost all stock mutual funds up with it. For example, on July 1, 1991, when the Dow jumped a startling 52 points, more than 98% of stock mutual funds were up for the day. Yet, of the more than 2,000 stocks that traded on the New York Stock Exchange, only 56% ended the day with a gain. The rest ended the day unchanged (21%) or actually fell in price (23%).

Advantage #6: Mutual funds' past performance is a matter of public record.

Advisory services, financial planners, and stockbrokers have records of past performance, but how public are they? And how were they computed? Did they include every recommendation made for every account? Mutual funds have fully disclosed performance histories, which are computed according to set standards. With a little research, you can learn exactly how the various mutual funds fared in relation to inflation or other investment alternatives.

Advantage #7: Mutual funds provide full-time professional management.

Highly trained investment specialists are hired to make

the decisions as to which stocks to buy. The person with the final decision-making authority is called the portfolio manager. He or she possesses expertise in many areas, including accounting, economics, and finance. He is experienced, hopefully having learned to avoid the common mistakes of the amateur investor. And most important, he is trained to have the self-discipline necessary to stick with the mutual fund's strategy even when events move against them for a time.

Advantage #8: Mutual funds allow you to efficiently reinvest your dividends.

If you were to spread $5,000 among five different stocks, your quarterly dividend checks might amount to $10 from each one. It's not possible to use such a small amount to buy more shares without paying very high relative commissions. Your mutual fund, however, will gladly reinvest any size dividends for you *automatically*. This can add significantly to your profits over several years.

Advantage #9: Mutual funds offer you automatic withdrawal plans.

Most funds let you automatically sell your shares in an amount and frequency of your choosing. This pre-planned selling enables the fund to mail you a check for a specified amount monthly or quarterly. This allows investors in stock funds that pay little or no dividends to receive periodic cash flow.

A GLIMPSE INTO A MUTUAL FUND PORTFOLIO

Most mutual funds report to their shareholders each quarter, providing market commentary, performance data, and a list of the fund's current holdings. Note that this growth fund is reporting that only 85% of its portfolio is invested in stocks. Most funds, even those dedicated to investing in stocks, will keep a small percentage of their holdings in CDs and Treasury bills to use for future purchases as well as to pay shareholders who wish to sell their fund shares on any given day.

Number of shares owned

COMMON STOCKS (85.3%)

Retail and Distribution (15.9%)			
Dayton-Hudson Corp.	205,000	$ 11,634	Current market value
Gap, Inc.	48,000	2,568	(in millions of dollars)
Liz Claiborne, Inc.	58,000	1,552	
Toys "R" Us, Inc.	568,000	14,413	
Wal Mart Stores,Inc.	548,000	15,618	
Walgreen Co.	180,000	8,212	
Group Total		53,997	
Consumer (13.2%)			
American Brands, Inc.	51,000	3,417	
Walt Disney Co.	16,000	1,638	
McDonald's Corp.	132,000	3,679	
PepsiCo. Inc.	197,000	14,775	
Philip Morris Co., Inc.	358,000	16,155	
Rubbermaid, Inc.	135,000	4,995	
Group Total		44,659	
Technology (6.4%)			
Automatic Data Processing, Inc.	247,000	12,443	
Computer Sciences Corp.	20,000	782	
MCI Communications Corp.	251,000	8,503	

Percent of the total portfolio that's invested in a particular industry or sector of the economy.

Advantage #10: Mutual funds provide you with individual attention.

It has been estimated that the average broker needs 400 accounts to make a living. How does he spread his time among those accounts? The common sense way would be to start with the largest accounts and work his way down. Where would that leave your $1,000 account? But in a mutual fund, the smallest member of the pool gets exactly the same attention as the largest because everybody is in it together.

Advantage #11: Mutual funds can be used for your IRA and other retirement plans.

Mutual funds offer accounts that can be used for IRAs, Keoghs, 401(k) plans, and even *rollovers* for when you take your retirement benefits from your corporate pension or profit-sharing plans. These accounts make it possible for you to transfer your pension benefits to an account under your control while protecting their tax-deferred status. They are also useful for combining several small IRAs into one large one.

Advantage #12: Mutual funds allow you to sell part or all of your shares at any time and get your money quickly.

By regulation, all mutual funds must redeem (buy back) their shares at their net asset value whenever you wish. It's usually as simple as a toll-free phone call. Of course, the amount you get back will be more or less than you initially put in, depending on how well the stocks in the portfolio have done during the time you were a part owner of the pool.

Advantage #13: Mutual funds enable you to instantly reduce the risk in your portfolio with just a phone call.

Most fund organizations (usually referred to as "families") allow investors to switch between their funds via a phone call and at no cost. One extremely popular application of this feature is to switch back and forth between a growth-oriented stock fund (during *bull markets*) and a more conservative income or money market fund (when the stock market weakens and a *bear market* threatens). This exchange feature enables you to act quickly on the basis of your stock market expectations.

Advantage #14: Mutual funds pay minimum commissions when buying and selling for the pool.

They buy stocks in such large quantities that they always qualify for the lowest brokerage commissions available. An average purchase of $1,000 of stock will cost the small investor $60 to buy and sell. That's a 6% commission charge. On the other hand, the cost is a mere fraction of 1% on a large purchase like $100,000. Many investors would show gains rather than losses if they could save 6% on every trade! The mutual-fund pool enjoys the savings from these massive volume discounts, enhancing the profitabilility of the pool. Eventually, then, part of that savings is yours. These commission savings, however, should not be confused with the annual operating expenses which every shareholder pays.

Advantage #15: Mutual funds provide safekeeping for your investment money.

All mutual funds are required to hire an independent bank or trust company to hold and account for all the cash and securities in the pool. This custodian has a legally binding responsibility to protect the interests of every shareholder. No mutual fund shareholder has ever lost money due to a mutual fund bankruptcy.

Advantage #16: Mutual funds handle your paperwork for you.

Capital gains and losses from the sale of stocks, as well as dividend and interest income earnings, are summarized into a report for each shareholder at the end of the year for tax purposes. Funds also manage the day-to-day chores such as dealing with transfer agents, handling stock certificates, reviewing brokerage confirmations, and more.

Bear Market is a market with falling prices of sufficient duration to indicate a downward trend.

Advantage #17: Mutual funds can be borrowed against in case of an emergency.

Although you hope it will never be necessary, you can use the value of your mutual fund holdings as collateral for a loan. If the need is short-term and you would rather not sell your funds because of tax or investment reasons, you can borrow against them rather than sell them.

Advantage #18: Mutual funds involve no personal liability beyond the investment risk in the portfolio.

Many investments, primarily partnerships and futures, require investors to sign papers wherein they agree to accept personal responsibility for certain liabilities generated by the undertaking. Thus, it is possible for investors to actually lose more money than they invest. This arrangement is generally indicative of speculative endeavors; I encourage you to avoid such arrangements. In contrast, mutual funds incur no personal risk.

Bull Market is a market with rising prices of sufficient duration to indicate an upward trend.

Advantage #19: Mutual fund advisory services are available that can greatly ease the research burden.

Due to the tremendous growth in the popularity of mutual fund investing, there has been a big jump in the number of investment newsletters that specialize in researching and writing about mutual funds. In the 1992 edition of *The Hulbert Guide to Financial Newsletters*, 41 were listed, and that just includes the ones that have been in existence since the beginning of 1989. Even within this group, there are different approaches. Some promote timing strategies that tell you when to buy and sell, others focus on just the funds at one of the giant organizations such as Fidelity and Vanguard, and others recommend balanced, diversified portfolios of mutual funds geared to your risk tolerance and stage of life. They usually offer a free issue upon request, publish once a month, and average $152 per year (although the majority range from $89 to $149) in cost.

Advantage #20: Mutual funds are heavily regulated by the SEC and have operated largely scandal-free for decades.

The fund industry is regulated by the *Securities & Exchange Commission* and is subject to the provisions of the Investment Company Act of 1940. The act requires that all mutual funds register with the SEC and that investors be given a prospectus, which must contain full information concerning the fund's history, operating policies, cost structure, and so on. Additionally, all funds use a bank that serves as the custodian of all the pool assets. This safeguard means the securities in the fund are protected from theft, fraud, and even the bankruptcy of the fund management organization itself. Of course, money can still be lost if poor investment decisions cause the value of the pool's investments to fall in value.

There are three primary ways you can profit from investing in mutual funds.

When you make your mutual fund investment you will receive shares to show exactly how much (that is, what portion) of the pool you own. The value of those shares fluctuates daily according to how well the investments in the pool are doing. For example, if the overall value of the stocks held in the pool goes up today, the value of the fund's shares will go up today, and vice versa. The greater the *volatility*, the greater the risk. The price you pay for your shares is based on the worth of the securities in the pool on the day you buy in. Typically, the *closing price* is used for establishing their market value. For this reason, mutual funds are usually bought or sold only at the day's closing prices. This means that it doesn't matter what time of day the fund receives your order—early or late—you'll still get that day's closing price.

You can profit from your shares in three primary ways. First, the dividends paid by the stocks in the portfolio will be paid out to you periodically, usually quarterly. Second, if the portfolio manager sells a stock for more than he paid for it originally, a capital gain results. These gains will also be paid out periodically, usually annually. And third, when you're ready to sell your shares in the pool, you might receive back more than you paid for them. ◆

--- IN A NUTSHELL ---

WITH MUTUAL FUNDS	WITH INDIVIDUAL STOCKS
1. The fund portfolio manager decides what stocks to buy and sell and when's the best time.	1. You decide what stocks to buy and sell and when's the best time.
2. You get the added safety that comes from diversifying among lots of different stocks.	2. You get the high-risk high-reward potential that comes from concentrating on just a handful of stocks.
3. You can invest any amount you want (above the minimum) and receive fractional shares.	3. Stock prices affect how much you can invest because you have to buy whole shares.
4. You can easily and efficiently reinvest all of your dividends.	4. It's difficult to reinvest all your dividends because the amounts are usually so small.
5. You can transfer your money between funds the same day.	5. It usually takes five business days to get your money when you sell.
6. You pay no sales charges when buying or selling no-load funds.	6. Even discount brokers' commissions can cost 1% each time you trade.

How Mutual Funds Are Sold and the Best Way to Buy Them

I. **There are two primary ways to go about investing in mutual funds.**

A. "Load" fund organizations sell their shares to investors through a sales network of brokers, insurance professionals, and financial planners. A percentage of every dollar you invest (which can run as high as 8½%) goes to the salesperson with whom you do business.

B. "No-load" fund organizations sell their shares to investors directly. They don't have a sales force to represent them, and so there need not be a "load" charged to the investor; 100% of every dollar invested goes to work in the investor's behalf.

II. **There are on-going costs associated with owning mutual fund shares.**

A. There are daily costs. All mutual funds charge for the portfolio manager's fee and other operating expenses. This is the way they make their money. The average charge is around 1% of the value of your investment per year.

B. There are other potential costs that *some* funds charge. These include marketing expenses, back-end loads, and exit fees. These are avoidable through selective shopping.

III. **Fund organizations vary in the excellence and variety of their funds as well as in the account minimums they require. You should select a fund organization based on the amount of money you have to start with and the kinds of investments you wish to focus on.**

A. If you have $2,000 or less to begin with, you must initially look for fund organizations with low account minimums.

B. As your portfolio grows in value, you will eventually want to open accounts with more than one fund organization in order to have a greater selection of funds to choose from.

C. For maximum convenience, flexibility, and selection, investigate the no-load fund services offered by The Charles Schwab Company and Fidelity Brokerage. I'll have more about these "cutting edge" services in Section 4.

What does it cost to buy mutual funds? That depends on how you buy them...

...whether you go to them or they come to you. Mutual funds earn their profits by the management fees they charge, which are based on the amount of money they are responsible for investing. The more investors' money they manage, the more they make. Naturally, they want to attract as many customers as possible.

So-called "load" funds get new customers by having a sales force of stockbrokers, financial planners, and insurance professionals sell their funds for them. These funds charge a sales fee, which is added on top of the fund's net asset value. This markup cost can run as high as 8½% on every dollar you invest. The load applies to all purchases you make in the fund, not just the first time; some load funds even charge to reinvest your dividends for you (which I think is going a bit far). In return, the salesperson comes up with recommendations as to which funds might be best suited for your goals and completes all the paperwork to get your account opened. The load is the way the salesperson is rewarded for opening and servicing new accounts. If you would never get around to doing the research needed to select funds that are right for you, the salesperson provides an important service by doing this work for you and motivating you to action.

There is another way. A great many mutual funds have

chosen to deal directly with investors. They don't have a sales force to represent them—they believe plenty of investors are willing to do their own research and paperwork in order to save on the sales load. *They don't come to you; you go to them.* Of course, they make it as easy as possible through their advertising, 800 numbers, and customer service departments. Since they don't have salespeople to pay, they don't charge the load (thus the name "no-load"). By showing some initiative, you can save the 3%-8½% load that is commonly charged. That means *all the money* you put into your fund account goes to work for *you.* I recommend you limit your investment shopping to no-load funds. You'll learn all you need to know in this booklet to select the funds that are right for you, and you'll save thousands of dollars in loads over the years.

But (I can hear many of you asking), what about investment performance? Isn't it true that load funds get better results than no-load funds?

Which kind has the better performance? The truth is they're pretty evenly matched. Neither group is inherently better than the other. One year several of the no-load categories will outperform their load counterparts. The next year it could well be the other way around. The following table shows how various load and no-load groups' performance compares over the past five and ten years. Notice that not only have they each had their share of winning results, but also how small the "margin of victory" usually is. They're so close that it's anyone's guess who will lead in performance in the coming year.

Both load and no-load fund organizations hire top professionals in an attempt to bolster their performance results, which are, after all, what they are selling. So why should you expect either type to be inherently superior to the other? You shouldn't.

LOAD VS. NO-LOAD MUTUAL FUND PERFORMANCE

OF FUNDS WITH AT LEAST A FIVE YEAR PERFORMANCE HISTORY FOR PERIODS ENDING 6/30/92

Risk Category	Number Of Funds	Avg 5 Yr Return	Avg 10 Yr Return
Small Company Funds: Load	36	7.7%	12.7%
Small Company Funds: No-Load	44	9.0%	15.1%
Growth Funds: Load	167	8.1%	15.5%
Growth Funds: No-Load	118	8.4%	15.6%
Growth & Income Funds: Load	97	8.5%	15.9%
Growth & Income Funds: No-Load	70	6.8%	13.6%
Equity Income Funds: Load	25	7.7%	15.2%
Equity Income Funds: No-Load	16	8.9%	15.7%

However, that doesn't mean that they're equally attractive. The load that investors pay comes out of their account up-front. In other words, they are "in the hole" the very day their account is opened. This means load funds *must* be consistently superior over time in order to overcome this drawback and provide higher returns than a comparable no-load fund. This places the burden of proof on the load funds.

What costs are involved in owning mutual funds?

● **Operating expenses.** These are charged by all mutual funds. They include the portfolio manager's fee, accounting and legal fees, and the cost of printing and mailing reports to the shareholders. The average is around 1% per year.

● **Marketing expenses.** These are charged by about one-half of all mutual funds, although they are predominantly favored by load funds (eight out of ten funds charging 12b-1 fees are sold through a sales network). They are referred to as 12b-1 fees because of the SEC ruling that permits them, and they can only be used to advertise and sell the fund to prospective investors. Most funds do not yet levy these charges, but it is a growing (and controversial) practice. They range from .10% to 1.25% annually.

● **Back-end loads, also sometimes called deferred sales charges.** These are most commonly assessed by funds affiliated with major brokerage firms. This approach allows the firms that use them to sell shares through their commissioned brokers without charging front-loads. The firm pays the brokers from these back-end loads and from the 12b-1 charges. Typically, if you sell during the first year, you are charged a back-end commission ranging from 4% to 6% of the amount originally invested. The percentage drops each year, gradually declining to zero after several years. They are deducted from your proceeds check when you pull your money out.

● **Exit fees.** Charged by a relatively few funds, these fees are intended either to discourage you from making frequent trades or to recoup the administrative costs associated with buying back your shares. Such fees can range from a flat $5.00 per withdrawal to as much as $1.00 for every $100 withdrawn. Like back-end loads, they are deducted from the check sent you at the time you sell your shares.

Summary. The first two categories, operating and marketing expenses, are deducted from the pool's value daily. Therefore, a fund's performance rating, which is based on the change in a pool's value over a period of time, already takes the effects of these costs into account. The mutual funds that I recommend in my monthly newsletter *Sound Mind Investing* have reasonable operating expenses; however, I generally do not recommend funds that charge front-end or back-end loads.

When you are ready to begin building your mutual fund portfolio, your "starting place" will primarily depend on how much you initially have available.

If you're just getting started, I suggest you consider either 20th Century or Invesco due to their willingness to take very small accounts. Fortunately, both are well run and have funds to choose from with outstanding performance records.

If you have at least $3,000 available for stock market investing...

...you will find your needs well met by choosing among the many no-load investment companies listed below. They are all reputable organizations that offer a variety of funds from which you can choose. They also allow you to move your money from one of their funds into another simply by making a toll-free phone call. As with all true no-load funds, there are no commissions charged to you, either when you invest or when you take your money out. These organizations provide you with a very cost-effective way to proceed with your program.

As your portfolio grows, you will want to diversify further. Although each of the above-mentioned organizations offers a variety of stock funds, you could run into either of two "problems." One, they might not offer a fund in the exact risk category or area of speciality you are seeking. Or, even if they do offer one, you might find that it is a relatively poor performer. At this point, it might be time to open a second mutual fund account at a different organization with strengths which complement those of your first organization and match up well with your current needs.

Leading No-Load Fund Families	
Benham	800-321-8321
Dreyfus	800-645-6561
Fidelity	800-544-8888
Invesco	800-525-8085
Neuberger	800-877-9700
Price	800-638-5660
Scudder	800-225-5163
SteinRoe	800-338-2550
20th Century	800-345-2021
Vanguard	800-662-7447

READING THE DAILY

These initials stand for Net Asset Value. Each day after the markets close, all of the investment securities owned by the pool are valued at that day's closing price. The total is then divided by the total number of shares in the pool in order to find out how much an individual share is worth. The value of an individual share is called its Net Asset Value and is the price at which shareholders were permitted to redeem (sell back) their shares on that day. The NAV continually fluctuates, depending on how the securities owned by the fund performed during the day. It also is affected by: (1) the costs of running the fund (2) 12b-1 marketing expenses, and (3) periodic distributions when the fund passes along capital gains, dividends, and interest to the shareholders.

The Offering Price is the price per share that new investors paid to buy into the fund on the previous day. For load funds, this price includes the sales markup. NL stands for No-Load, meaning there is no sales markup; new investors pay the Net Asset Value for their shares. Although there is no front-end load, there may be back-end loads or exit fees.

	NAV	Offer Price	NAV Chg.
AAL Mutual:			
CaGr p	10.64	11.17	-.14
Inco p	9.43	9.90	-.01
MuBd p	9.85	10.34	-.02
AARP Invest:			
CaGr	25.94	NL	-.51
GiniM	14.94	NL	-.03
GthInc	23.19	NL	-.26
HQ Bd	14.63	NL	-.04
TxFBd	16.38	NL	-.08
TxFSh	15.15	NL	-.01
ABT Funds:			
Emrg p	8.48	8.90	-.14
Gthln p	8.76	9.20	-.14
Secln p	9.38	9.85	-.04
Utilln p	11.95	12.55	-.12
AHA Bal	10.11	NL	-.07
AdsnCa p	16.81	17.33	-.24
ADTEK	9.00	9.00	-.16
AFA NAv	9.91	10.40	-.17
AFA Tele	14.62	15.35	-.41
AIM Funds:			
Chart p	6.80	7.20	-.08
Const p	7.56	8.00	-.20
CvYld p	9.84	10.33	-.17
HiYld p	6.32	6.64	-.03
LimM p	9.79	9.96	......
Sumit	7.68	8.33	-.14

The names in bold type indicate a fund organization that has several funds it operates. Such groups of mutual funds are called fund "families." It is quite easy to move your investments from one fund to another within the same family, usually with just a phone call. This makes the larger no-load fund families, such as Vanguard and Price, more attractive because they have such a large variety of funds from which to choose.

MUTUAL FUND LISTINGS

	NAV	**Offer Price**	**NAV Chg.**
Carnegie Funds:			
Govt p	9.07	9.50	-.01
TEOhG	9.07	9.50	-.02
TENHi	9.55	10.11	-.01
Cardnl	10.00	10.93	-.15
CrdnlGv	8.73	9.17	-.01
Cnt Shs	17.25	NL	-.23
ChpHY p	10.92	11.46	-.02
Chestnt	91.90	NL	-1.68
CIGNA Funds:			
Agrsv p	12.18	12.82	-.34
GvSc p	9.81	10.33	-.01
Grth p	13.33	14.03	-.24
HiYld p	8.39	8.83	-.04
Inco p	7.36	7.75	-.02
MunB p	7.67	8.07	-.03
Util p	12.37	13.02	-.20
Value p	14.83	15.61	-.34
Citibank IRA-CIT:			
Balan f	2.18	NL	-.03
Equit f	2.37	NL	-.04
Incom f	1.98	NL	-.01
ShtTr f	1.70	NL	......
Clipper	37.57	37.57	-.66
Colonial Funds:			
AGold p	21.08	22.37	+.17
CalTE	6.94	7.29	-.02
CpCsh p	41.68	42.53	-.20

NAV Chg. This column shows the per share change in the value of the fund from the previous day. Small rises and dips are normal and should not cause undue concern. In weekly mutual fund listings, such as those found in Barron's and many Sunday papers, this column will reflect the change for the entire week. A string of declines over several weeks during which similar funds are climbing is an early warning sign that a change may be needed.

The name of each fund is listed in normal type. Often you can tell what the fund's special emphasis is by its name. The abbreviations can be puzzling at first. Here's how to decipher some of those appearing in the AARP listing: CaGr stands for capital growth, GthInc indicates a growth and income fund, HQBd is their high quality bond fund, TxFBd is their tax-free bond fund, and TxFSh is also a tax-free bond fund, but with a short-term portfolio. In the CIGNA family: Agrsv is their high-risk aggressive growth stock fund, HiYld is a high yield (junk) bond fund, and Util is a fund which specializes in utility stocks.

Many of the funds have single letters following their names. These are codes to convey something extra you should know about that fund. The most common code letters are:

" f " yesterday's price was not available by press time, so the price from the day before is still being used; " p " 12b-1 marketing costs are paid from the pool's assets; " n " no front-end load or contingent deferred sales load is charged; " d " today's NAV is a new 52-week low; " u " today's NAC is a new 52-week high; " r " redemption costs (exit fees) are charged under certain circumstances, and " x " today's NAV was reduced by the amount of a dividend soon to be paid out to shareholders.

Another alternative is to open an investment account at either the Charles Schwab Company or Fidelity Brokerage Services.

In addition to stocks and bonds, they each offer a no-load mutual fund service unmatched by any other broker. These services allow you to quickly and easily buy/sell no-load mutual fund shares for your account without having to open separate accounts at all the various fund organizations. They perform this service *commission-free on some funds* or for a small charge for others.

Why pay for this when you can go to a no-load organization and buy its fund shares for free? Greater convenience, for one (see opposite page). And greater selection for another. Because Schwab and Fidelity offer hundreds of different funds to choose from, many of them will be superior performers to those of the one or two no-load organizations where you might have accounts (especially in the stock fund categories). In view of the far greater convenience and variety of funds, these services constitute the "new look" of fund investing for the Nineties. We'll take a closer look in Section 4.

Of course, if you wish to deal directly with each fund organization, then do so. It might take a little longer, but the end result is the same. ♦

STEPS NEEDED TO MOVE YOUR MONEY FROM ONE MUTUAL FUND ORGANIZATION TO ANOTHER

Why go through a brokerage firm like Schwab and pay them to do what you can do for yourself? The answer is simple: convenience when moving your investment dollars from one mutual fund organization to a new one where you don't already have an account. For example, let's pretend that you want to sell your shares at Organization A and invest the money in one of the funds at Organization B. If you weren't using Schwab's mutual fund service, here's what you'd need to do:

❑ Mail written instructions to Organization A (with your signature guaranteed by your local bank or broker) to sell your shares.

❑ Wait seven to ten days for your proceeds check to arrive from Organization A.

❑ While you're waiting, contact Organization B and ask them to send you the new account application forms.

❑ When they arrive, complete the forms.

❑ Mail them to Organization B with your check to pay for the new fund shares you want to purchase.

❑ Finally, wait two to three days before you know your order has been processed. (What's been happening in the stock market while you're doing all this waiting is anyone's guess!)

The Great Variety of Mutual Funds: The Choices Are Almost Limitless

I. **Mutual funds can be categorized into risk groups according to their stated objectives and investment strategies.**

   A. Funds that invest only in stocks are called equity funds. These are the funds to use when you wish to "invest by owning" and are generally higher risk in nature.

   B. Funds that invest only in bonds are called fixed-income funds. These are the funds to use when you wish to "invest by lending" and are generally lower risk in nature.

II. **The mutual fund industry offers a tremendous array of choices.**

   A. There are dozens of mutual fund organizations to choose from, each with its own particular strengths. For some their strength is stock funds, others their bond funds. For some, it's just the extensive variety they offer.

   B. The variety of choices, even at one organization, can be huge. The two largest groups,

3

Fidelity and Vanguard, offer 180 and 60 different funds, respectively.

III. Index funds invest in a particular group of stocks or bonds, which constitute a market index. If you don't want to deal with a number of funds in putting together your portfolio, an index fund is a prudent and economical alternative.

The mutual fund industry is the fastest growing industry in the U.S. It is estimated that about 50 million investors...

...have placed more than one trillion dollars in America's more than 3,000 mutual funds. The sheer number and variety of funds has caused investors to be confused about what is available, let alone what is appropriate.

The place to begin is to understand that mutual funds are placed into groupings—called risk categories—according to what their stated goals are. Unfortunately, it turns out that there are no "official" categories that all analysts and rating services can agree on and use uniformly. Even if there were, picking a permanent category for a fund can be tricky. There are times when a fund's real-life portfolio differs from what its name might suggest. For example, as it grows a fund might move outside its primary area of interest because it can't find enough attractive investments there. Or, the investment climate might cause a fund to hold more money market securities than usual because stocks seem overvalued.

A key resource I use to study the different kinds of mutual funds, evaluate their performance, and classify them according to risk...

...is the mutual fund database provided by Morningstar, one of the country's two leading mutual fund reporting services (the other is Lipper Analytical). Morningstar places every mutual fund into one of three major camps: equity (stock) funds, fixed-income (bond) funds, and hybrid (a mix of both stock and bonds) funds. Within each camp, there are many risk categories. A lot can be known about how risky a mutual fund is just by understanding how to use a risk classification system.

Brokers and media commentators routinely encourage you to seek higher returns but downplay the reminder that "higher risk" is involved. The real possibility that you could ever have to deal with the consequences of accepting greater risk is presented as an abstraction, not related to your everyday experience. Actually losing part or all of your money in an investment is something that happens to the "other guy," sort of like getting cancer. I want to be certain that when you consider accepting a higher risk, you mentally translate that in your mind to: "Hey, I'd better stop and think. This means I stand a very real chance of actually losing some of my money. Can I afford that?" A discussion of risk should not come across as academic and impersonal.

Think of mutual funds as offering the convenience of something you're pretty familiar with: eating out! Someone else has done all the work of...

...developing the recipes, shopping for quality at the best prices, and cooking and assembling the dinners so that foods that go well together are served in the right proportions.

THINK OF THE FUND ORGANIZATION AS BEING THE RESTAURANT...

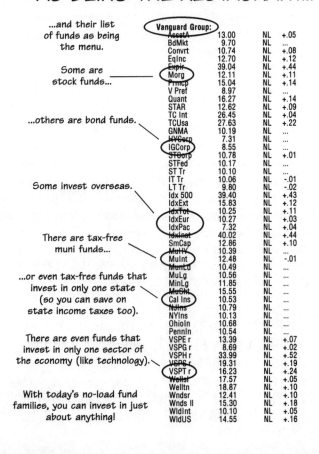

...and their list of funds as being the menu.

Some are stock funds...

...others are bond funds.

Some invest overseas.

There are tax-free muni funds...

...or even tax-free funds that invest in only one state (so you can save on state income taxes too).

There are even funds that invest in only one sector of the economy (like technology).

With today's no-load fund families, you can invest in just about anything!

Vanguard Group:

AssetA	13.00	NL	+.05
BdMkt	9.70	NL	...
Convrt	10.74	NL	+.08
EqInc	12.70	NL	+.12
Explr	39.04	NL	+.44
Morg	12.11	NL	+.11
Prmcp	15.04	NL	+.14
V Pref	8.97	NL	...
Quant	16.27	NL	+.14
STAR	12.62	NL	+.09
TC Int	26.45	NL	+.04
TCUsa	27.63	NL	+.22
GNMA	10.19	NL	...
HYCorp	7.31	NL	...
IGCorp	8.55	NL	...
STCorp	10.78	NL	+.01
STFed	10.17	NL	...
ST Tr	10.10	NL	...
IT Tr	10.06	NL	-.01
LT Tr	9.80	NL	-.02
Idx 500	39.40	NL	+.43
IdxExt	15.83	NL	+.12
IdxTot	10.25	NL	+.11
IdxEur	10.27	NL	+.03
IdxPac	7.32	NL	+.04
Idxinst	40.02	NL	+.44
SmCap	12.86	NL	+.10
MuHY	10.39	NL	...
MuInt	12.48	NL	-.01
MunLtd	10.49	NL	...
MuLg	10.56	NL	...
MinLg	11.85	NL	...
MuSht	15.55	NL	...
Cal Ins	10.53	NL	...
NJIns	10.79	NL	...
NYIns	10.13	NL	...
OhioIn	10.68	NL	...
PennIn	10.54	NL	...
VSPE r	13.39	NL	+.07
VSPG r	8.69	NL	+.02
VSPH r	33.99	NL	+.52
VSPS r	19.31	NL	+.19
VSPT r	16.23	NL	+.24
Wellsl	17.57	NL	+.05
Welltn	18.87	NL	+.10
Wndsr	12.41	NL	+.10
Wnds II	15.30	NL	+.18
WldInt	10.10	NL	+.05
WldUS	14.55	NL	+.16

For mutual funds, that's the job of the professional portfolio manager—he develops his strategy, shops for the right securities at the best prices, and then assembles the portfolio with an appropriate amount of diversification. And the analogy doesn't stop there. Just as there are many different dinner entrees to choose from at most nice restaurants (such as steak, seafood, chicken, pasta, and so on), there are also many kinds of mutual funds to choose from at most fund organizations. Each kind has its own "flavor."

The graphic at left is the listing for Vanguard, which appears daily in the mutual fund section of the newspaper. Vanguard is one of the giants in the no-load fund industry and offers quite a "menu" for its investors. The point here is simply to show you *how many different funds you can find at a single fund organization.*

Want a conservative blue chip stock fund? Try Windsor. Perhaps something a little more aggressive? Check out Explorer or one of their global funds. Prefer bonds instead? They've got funds that specialize in corporates, governments, and tax-frees. Want short-term bonds instead of long-term? No problem—they offer funds that have different portfolio maturities for all three bond categories.

The trend among fund organizations is to offer investors a choice in just about every investing specialty and risk group imaginable.

But what if all these choices, rather than making your life easier, only intimidate you?

When faced with too many choices, do you "freeze up"? If so, then perhaps you should consider using an "index fund" as your primary investing vehicle. An index fund is *a special kind of mutual fund that has only one objective: to mirror the performance of a market index* such as Standard & Poor's 500 Stock Index or the Wilshire 5000. The portfolio manager invests in the same securities that are used in calculating the index. The fund will make or lose money to the same extent the index after which it is patterned shows gains or losses. For example, if the S&P 500 gains 15% in a given year, then any S&P 500 index fund should also gain about 15% that year. From an investing point of view, what could be simpler?

The growth in the number and size of index funds has been explosive in recent years, thanks to the interest shown by pension funds, insurance companies, and other big institutional investors. More than $275 billion has been invested in index funds, and 75% of that is invested in S&P 500-type index funds because it is still the benchmark most investors compare themselves against. All of this "smart" money going into index funds shows how difficult it can be to outperform the market. If it were a simple matter to know how to invest in the right stocks (or bonds) at the right time, everyone would be wealthy. An investment in an index fund is another way of saying, "It is so hard to consistently do better than the market averages! I'll give up the potential to make *more* than the overall market in return for the knowledge that I won't make *less*." The graphs on the next page, based on the performance results from 424 stock-oriented mutual funds, tell the story.

The primary reasons for their popularity are twofold:

❶ **To guard against sub-par investment returns.** Pretend you're a portfolio manager at a large company like General Motors, and your job performance is evaluated primarily on how well your investments do each year compared to the S&P 500. Although you might not gain more than the S&P, you surely wouldn't want to do worse! Hence the attractiveness of index funds: to help assure that your results are in line with those of the general market.

❷ **To lower investment expenses and commissions.** The average stock fund incurs operating expenses each year of around 1.5% *on top of* the commissions the mutual fund pays when it buys and sells within the pool. Commissions add another 1% to 2% to overhead annually, depending on how active the portfolio manager is in buying and selling. All of this comes out of the shareholders' profits. Index funds, on the other hand, are very inexpensive to operate and administer; for instance, Vanguard's index funds (both stock and bond) typically incur total expenses and commissions of .5% or less per year.

The primary point I want you to understand is...

...that many no-load mutual funds organizations operate a wide variety of funds from which you can choose when putting together your portfolio. And if you don't want to bother trying to pick the ones that will "do the best," then

WHAT PERCENTAGE OF STOCK FUNDS HAVE PERFORMED BETTER THAN THE S&P 500 INDEX?

I analyzed the performance results of several hundred stock funds, load and no-load, to see how well they were doing in comparision to the S&P 500. The results are shown on the bar graphs below, with the performance of the S&P 500 index marked by the vertical line.

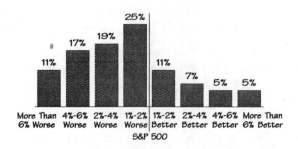

FOR 3 YEARS ENDING 6/30/92

This graph shows that only 28% of the funds (sum of percentages to the right of the vertical line) were able to outperform the S&P while 72% of the funds (shown left of the vertical line) underperformed the index. In spite of all their knowledge and experience, the professional portfolio managers as a group found it difficult to do better than the general market.

they also offer index funds that will provide returns roughly equal to the overall market. It's like walking through the cafeteria line: great variety at reasonable prices. And there is also a great variety to choose *among organizations*. Your choices are almost limitless. Now, let's go shopping! ◆

This second graph covers a full decade, and confirms what we suspected from the first one: it's difficult to consistently outperform the market, and the longer the time period being measured, the more difficult it is.

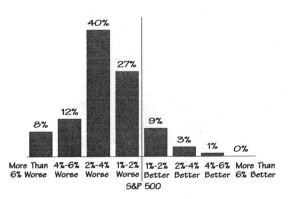

FOR 10 YEARS ENDING 6/30/92
For the full 10 year period, only 13% of funds could do better than the S&P 500. We also see that the longer the time period, the more the funds move toward the center of the graph, that is, the more they tend to be "average." Also, it gets increasingly difficult to outperform the market by a significant amount—none of the funds were able to beat the S&P by 6% per year.

Schwab and Fidelity: No-Load Fund Investing For The Nineties

I. In addition to buying no-load funds from the individual fund organizations, they can also be purchased through certain discount brokers.

II. The first discount broker to offer no-load funds was the Charles Schwab Company.

A. The Mutual Fund Marketplace is the name for their service where you can buy and sell certain no-load fund shares. There is a small commission for these transactions.

B. Schwab also offers Mutual Fund OneSource, a service that lets you buy or sell from a list of more than 200 no-load funds *without paying a commission*. The funds on the list are called "No Transaction Fee" (NTF) funds.

III. Fidelity, the giant mutual fund organization, offers a competing service similar to Schwab's OneSource called Funds Network.

A. The advantage of the Funds Network is that a large number of Fidelity's own funds are available through it on a No Transaction Fee basis. All Fidelity funds purchased through Schwab OneSource carry a transaction fee.

B. The disadvantage of the Funds Network is that it doesn't offer as many funds from as many organizations as does Schwab OneSource.

IV. The greater convenience and variety of these services coupled with their No Transaction Fee policy makes them the best choice for most investors who wish to use no-load funds.

The great thing about no-load funds...

...is that you can put together just about any kind of portfolio you want without paying the usual broker's commissions. You can even have accounts at several organizations in order to have access to most of the top-performers.

However, along with having such a variety of choice comes housekeeping chores that can be inconvenient and occasionally confusing. You've got multiple sets of 800 numbers, application forms, investment account numbers, different organizational policies, and monthly statements to contend with. When you want to sell shares at one organization and buy them at another, you've got to wait for a check from the first fund before sending your check off to the next one. And then there's all the tax information to keep track of.

To relieve you of this hassle, the Charles Schwab Company pioneered its Mutual Fund Marketplace a few years back. For a small service fee, Schwab offered access to hundreds of no-load funds through one investment account. It wasn't long before Fidelity, the giant mutual fund organization, came along to one-up Schwab by offering the same service with even more funds to choose from.

Schwab struck back with its OneSource service which *eliminated the service fees completely for certain fund families*. In 1993, Fidelity responded by introducing a similar no-transaction-fee service of its own. Both of these companies are now battling it out to see which one can sign up the most funds and thereby offer the widest selection. Free competition in the marketplace has once again resulted in better and less costly service for investors!

Now you can choose from roughly 200 "no transaction fee" no-load funds at either organization. The table at right gives you the fund lineups at the time this was written, but be advised that new funds are being added all the time. With one toll-free call (to phone lines that are answered 24 hours a day), you can make changes in your portfolio. You'll get one

Mutual Funds Offered with No Transaction Fees	Fidelity Funds Network	Schwab One Source
Benham	23	22
Berger	2	2
Dreyfus	30	37
Evergreen	11	11
Fidelity	68	No
Founders	8	10
IAI Funds	No	12
Invesco	No	23
Janus	12	12
Lexington	No	11
NeubergerBerman	8	9
Schwab	No	9
Skyline	No	3
SteinRoe	11	11
Strong	13	14
TwentiethCentury	No	10
Other	0	33
Total	186	229

monthly statement that includes your transaction history, dividends, and the current market values for all your holdings. Plus, both Schwab and Fidelity offer their clients free performance reports that include helpful data on all the funds they offer and are completely updated every three months.

It's time to do some window shopping! You may not be ready to actually buy anything yet...

...but it'd be good for you to walk through the mutual fund mall and become familiar with the businesses there. Following are samplings of some of the 200+ no-load funds available through either the Schwab or Fidelity mutual fund services that can be bought or sold without paying any commissions or transaction fees. I've listed some of the leading stock (pages 52-53), bond (pages 54-55), and international funds (pages 56-57) over the past three years.

When you compare mutual fund performance...

...it's important to compare "apples with apples." That means comparing a fund's performance primarily to other funds that have similar objectives and are taking similar risks. In other words, only with its immediate peer group. The graphic at far right explains the peer group definitions (frequently called "investment objectives") that are most commonly found in the investment industry when categorizing stock funds. These are the terms you'll encounter when reading financial magazines and newspapers, and so I've grouped the funds accordingly.

The "3 Year Annualized Return" column in the following tables shows what the fund returned, on average, over each of the past three years (for the period ending March 31, 1994). Some of the newer funds in the fast-growing international area do not yet have three year histories.

I've also included the minimum investment required to open an account in each fund. These differ from fund to fund because each organization sets its own minimums.

These listings are not complete—there are many more funds I could have included. I selected these to show you the quality and breadth of funds available on a no-load, no transaction fee basis through the Schwab/Fidelity services. This introduction is just to whet your appetite! For more on Schwab OneSource, call 800-266-5623, and for Fidelity's Funds-Network, call 800-544-9697.

THE MAJOR CLASSIFICATIONS FOR STOCK FUNDS

Aggressive Growth Funds

Seek maximum capital gains. Some may invest in stocks of businesses that are somewhat out of the mainstream, and may also use specialized investing techniques such as option-writing, short-selling and short-term trading.

Growth Funds

invest in the common stocks of well-established companies. Their primary aim is to produce an increase in the value of their investments (capital gains) rather than a flow of dividends.

Growth & Income Funds

invest mainly in the common stock of companies that have had increasing share value but also a solid record of paying dividends. This type of fund attempts to combine long-term capital growth with a steady stream of income.

Equity Income Funds

Seek a high level of current income by investing in equity securities of companies with good dividend-paying records.

Fund Name	Investment Objective	3 Year Annual Return	Minimum Initial Purchase
Invesco Dynamics	Aggressive Growth	31.1%	$ 1,000
SteinRoe Capital Opportunity	Aggressive Growth	28.6%	1,000
Strong Discovery	Aggressive Growth	27.8%	1,000
Founders Special	Aggressive Growth	27.2%	1,000
20th Century Giftrust Investors	Small Companies	42.1%	250
20th Century Ultra Investors	Small Companies	32.0%	1,000
Founders Discovery	Small Companies	27.5%	1,000
Founders Frontier	Small Companies	23.8%	1,000
Neuberger & Berman Genesis	Small Companies	23.1%	1,000
Dreyfus New Leaders	Small Companies	23.0%	2,500
Evergreen Limited Market	Small Companies	22.2%	5,000
20th Century Vista Investors	Small Companies	21.5%	1,000
Berger 100	Growth Funds	35.4%	250
Fidelity Retirement Growth	Growth Funds	25.3%	500
Founders Growth	Growth Funds	24.5%	1,000
Fidelity Trend	Growth Funds	23.8%	2,500
Fidelity Value	Growth Funds	23.4%	2,500
Strong Opportunity	Growth Funds	23.3%	1,000
SteinRoe Special	Growth Funds	22.6%	1,000
20th Century Heritage Investors	Growth Funds	21.7%	1,000
Neuberger & Berman Sel Sectors	Growth Funds	20.6%	1,000
Fidelity Disciplined Equity	Growth Funds	20.6%	2,500
Invesco Growth	Growth Funds	20.3%	1,000
Neuberger & Berman Manhattan	Growth Funds	19.2%	1,000
Janus Fund	Growth Funds	19.2%	1,000
20th Century Growth Investors	Growth Funds	18.8%	1,000
Neuberger & Berman Partners	Growth Funds	18.8%	1,000

SAMPLING OF NO-LOAD STOCK FUNDS FROM SCHWAB/FIDELITY

Fund Name	Investment Objective	3 Year Annual Return	Minimum Initial Purchase
Berger 101	Growth & Income	27.8%	$ 250
Neuberger & Berman Guardian	Growth & Income	22.3%	1,000
Benham Income & Growth	Growth & Income	18.6%	1,000
Strong Total Return	Growth & Income	18.1%	250
SteinRoe Prime Equities	Growth & Income	18.0%	1,000
Evergreen Value Timing	Growth & Income	17.9%	2,000
Fidelity Fund	Growth & Income	16.8%	2,500
Lexington Growth & Income	Growth & Income	16.7%	1,000
Lexington Corporate Leaders	Growth & Income	15.5%	1,000
Fidelity Market Index	Growth & Income	15.3%	2,500
Dreyfus Peoples Index	Growth & Income	15.3%	2,500
Evergreen American Retirement	Growth & Income	14.9%	2,000
Fidelity Equity-Income II	Equity Income	27.5%	2,500
Invesco Industrial Income	Equity Income	19.9%	1,000
SteinRoe Total Return	Equity Income	16.2%	1,000
Evergreen Total Return	Equity Income	15.2%	2,000
Invesco Strategic Gold	Precious Metals	13.7%	1,000
Benham Gold Equities Index	Precious Metals	13.7%	1,000
Lexington Goldfund	Precious Metals	11.7%	1,000
Invesco Strategic Financial Svcs.	Sector Fund	37.8%	1,000
Invesco Strategic Leisure	Sector Fund	36.8%	1,000
Invesco Strategic Technology	Sector Fund	34.2%	1,000
Evergreen Global Real Estate	Sector Fund	23.6%	2,000
Fidelity Real Estate Investment	Sector Fund	23.2%	2,500
Invesco Strategic Utilities	Sector Fund	19.8%	1,000
Invesco Strategic Health Science	Sector Fund	14.6%	1,000

Fund Name	Investment Objective	3 Year Annual Return	Minimum Initial Purchase
Dreyfus A Bonds Plus	High Quality Corp Bonds	13.9%	$ 2,500
IAI Bond Fund	High Quality Corp Bonds	12.1%	5,000
20th Century Long-Term Bond	High Quality Corp Bonds	11.0%	10,000
Fidelity Intermediate Bond	High Quality Corp Bonds	10.6%	2,500
SteinRoe Intermediate Bond	High Quality Corp Bonds	10.5%	1,000
Neuberger & Berman Ltd. Matur.	High Quality Corp Bonds	7.9%	2,000
Neuberger & Berman Ultra Short	High Quality Corp Bonds	4.7%	2,000
Fidelity Investment Grade Bond	Various Quality Corps	14.2%	2,500
Strong Income	Various Quality Corps	13.6%	1,000
Invesco Select Income	Various Quality Corps	13.4%	1,000
SteinRoe Income	Various Quality Corps	13.1%	1,000
Strong Short-Term Bond	Various Quality Corps	10.2%	1,000
Fidelity Short-Term Bond	Various Quality Corps	9.9%	2,500
Strong Advantage	Various Quality Corps	9.0%	1,000
Fidelity Capital & Income	High Yield "Junk" Bonds	27.3%	2,500
Fidelity Spartan High-Income	High Yield "Junk" Bonds	25.5%	10,000
Invesco High-Yield	High Yield "Junk" Bonds	17.9%	1,000
Skyline Monthly Income	High Yield "Junk" Bonds	16.8%	1,000
Fidelity Spartan Long-Term	U.S. Government	13.9%	10,000
Strong Government Securities	U.S. Government	12.9%	1,000
Fidelity Government Securities	U.S. Government	11.8%	2,500
Invesco U.S. Govt. Securities	U.S. Government	10.5%	1,000
Founders Government Securities	U.S. Government	9.8%	1,000
Fidelity Spartan Govt. Income	U.S. Government	9.6%	10,000
SteinRoe Government Income	U.S. Government	9.3%	1,000
Dreyfus S/I Government	U.S. Government	9.2%	2,500

SAMPLING OF NO-LOAD BOND FUNDS FROM SCHWAB/FIDELITY

◆ 55 ◆

Fund Name	Investment Objective	3 Year Annual Return	Minimum Initial Purchase
Benham GNMA Income	Govt-Backed Mortgages	9.8%	$ 1,000
Dreyfus Investors GNMA	Govt-Backed Mortgages	9.6%	2,500
Lexington GNMA Income	Govt-Backed Mortgages	9.6%	1,000
Dreyfus GNMA	Govt-Backed Mortgages	9.3%	2,500
Fidelity Spartan Ginnie Mae	Govt-Backed Mortgages	8.8%	10,000
Fidelity Ginnie Mae	Govt-Backed Mortgages	8.7%	2,500
Fidelity Mortgage Securities	Govt-Backed Mortgages	8.1%	2,500
General Municipal Bond	Tax-Free Municipals	12.6%	2,500
Strong Municipal Bond	Tax-Free Municipals	12.4%	2,500
Benham Natl. T/F Long-Term	Tax-Free Municipals	12.1%	1,000
Fidelity Spartan Muni Income	Tax-Free Municipals	11.7%	10,000
Fidelity Aggressive Tax-Free	Tax-Free Municipals	11.4%	2,500
Fidelity Municipal Bond	Tax-Free Municipals	11.2%	2,500
Invesco Tax-Free L/T Bond	Tax-Free Municipals	11.1%	1,000
Dreyfus Municipal Bond	Tax-Free Municipals	11.0%	2,500
Fidelity Insured Tax-Free	Tax-Free Municipals	11.0%	2,500
20th Century T/E Long-Term	Tax-Free Municipals	10.6%	10,000
Dreyfus Insured Muni Bond	Tax-Free Municipals	10.5%	2,500
Fidelity High-Yield Tax-Free	Tax-Free Municipals	10.4%	2,500
Dreyfus Intermediate Municipal	Tax-Free Municipals	10.4%	2,500
SteinRoe Managed Municipals	Tax-Free Municipals	10.4%	1,000
Fidelity Limited-Term Municipal	Tax-Free Municipals	10.4%	2,500
SteinRoe Intermediate Municipal	Tax-Free Municipals	9.7%	1,000
Benham Natl. T/F Intermediate	Tax-Free Municipals	9.6%	1,000
Lexington Tax-Exempt Bond	Tax-Free Municipals	9.1%	1,000
20th Century T/E Intermediate	Tax-Free Municipals	8.8%	10,000
SteinRoe High-Yield Municipal	Tax-Free Municipals	8.5%	1,000
Neuberger & Berman Municipal	Tax-Free Municipals	8.5%	2,000

Fund Name	Investment Objective	3 Year Annual Return	Minimum Initial Purchase
Scudder Short-Term Global Inc	ST World Income	6.5%	$ 1,000
Blanchard Short-Term Global Inc	ST World Income	5.1%	3,000
Alliance World Income	ST World Income	3.9%	10,000
Fidelity Short-Term World Inc	ST World Income	new	2,500
Scudder International Bond	Worldwide Bonds	13.2%	1,000
Bull & Bear Global Income	Worldwide Bonds	13.1%	1,000
T. Rowe Price Intl Bond	Worldwide Bonds	13.0%	2,500
Warburg Pincus Global Fixed Inc	Worldwide Bonds	11.4%	2,500
T. Rowe Price Global Govt	Worldwide Bonds	7.7%	2,500
Fidelity Global Bond	Worldwide Bonds	7.6%	2,500
Loomis Sayles Global Bond	Worldwide Bonds	new	1,000
Benham European Govt Bond	Worldwide Bonds	new	1,000
Fidelity New Markets Income	Worldwide Bonds	new	2,500
Founders Worldwide Growth	Worldwide Stocks	13.9%	1,000
Scudder Global	Worldwide Stocks	12.7%	1,000
Lexington Global	Worldwide Stocks	10.7%	1,000
Bull & Bear U.S. & Overseas	Worldwide Stocks	9.4%	1,000
Janus Worldwide	Worldwide Stocks	new	1,000
Robertson Stephens Contrarian	Worldwide Stocks	new	5,000
Montgomery Global Opportunity	Worldwide Stocks	new	500
Scudder Global Small Company	Worldwide Stocks	new	1,000
Lexington Worldwide Emerg Mkt	Foreign Stocks	16.6%	1,000
Olympic International	Foreign Stocks	15.6%	10,000
Warburg Pincus Intl Equity Comm	Foreign Stocks	15.4%	2,500
USAA Investment Intl	Foreign Stocks	14.7%	1,000
Bartlett Value International	Foreign Stocks	12.7%	5,000

Fund Name	Investment Objective	3 Year Annual Return	Minimum Initial Purchase
T. Rowe Price Intl Stock	Foreign Stocks	12.6%	$ 2,500
Babson-Stewart Ivory Intl	Foreign Stocks	12.3%	2,500
Vontobel EuroPacific	Foreign Stocks	12.2%	1,000
IAI International	Foreign Stocks	11.6%	5,000
Scudder International	Foreign Stocks	10.3%	1,000
Vanguard International Growth	Foreign Stocks	10.1%	3,000
Vanguard/Trustees' Equity Intl	Foreign Stocks	9.0%	10,000
Invesco International Growth	Foreign Stocks	4.1%	1,000
Fidelity Latin America	Foreign Stocks	new	2,500
20th Century Intl Equity	Foreign Stocks	new	1,000
Strong International Stock	Foreign Stocks	new	1,000
Columbia International Stock	Foreign Stocks	new	1,000
Montgomery Intl Small Cap	Foreign Stocks	new	500
Dreyfus International Equity	Foreign Stocks	new	2,500
Montgomery Emerging Mkts	Foreign Stocks	new	500
Oakmark International	Foreign Stocks	new	2,500
Founders Passport	Foreign Stocks	new	1,000
T. Rowe Price European Stock	European Stocks	8.7%	2,500
Invesco European	European Stocks	7.0%	1,000
United Services European Inc	European Stocks	0.5%	1,000
Skyline Europe	European Stocks	new	1,000
T. Rowe Price New Asia	Pacific Stocks	16.8%	2,500
Invesco Pacific Basin	Pacific Stocks	7.1%	1,000
Japan	Pacific Stocks	4.6%	1,000
Scudder Pacific Opportunity	Pacific Stocks	new	1,000
T. Rowe Price Japan	Pacific Stocks	new	2,500
Fidelity Southeast Asia	Pacific Stocks	new	2,500

Income Taxes and Your Mutual Fund Investments

5

I. Mutual funds are simply conduits through which you invest. The capital gains and losses and dividend and interest income they receive are treated as if they were yours personally.

   A. Investment companies periodically pay to their shareholders the interest and dividends the funds receive on their investments.

   B. Investment companies periodically pay to their shareholders the capital gains the funds make when selling their investments.

   C. The date that these distributions are set aside from the fund's assets for payment to shareholders is called the "ex-dividend" date. This is the significant date as far as income taxes are concerned, not the later date on which you receive the distribution check in the mail.

II. The tax accounting for mutual funds can be confusing, even to veteran investors.

   A. Buying just prior to a fund distribution does not result in an actual gain, but merely results in incurring an immediate tax liability.

B. Distributions are taxable in the year they are declared, not in the year they are received by the investor.

C. There are two kinds of capital gains to keep in mind—those the funds can earn by buying and selling within the fund portfolios, and those investors can earn by selling their fund shares for more than they paid for them.

D. The IRS recognizes three different methods for computing capital gains on fund shares. If you sell part (rather than all) of your shares in a fund, you can select the one that results in the lowest tax liability.

III. Timing your selling so as to minimize or postpone your tax liability is a natural inclination; however, it should not supersede the normal common sense disciplines built into your long-term strategy.

If you're tempted to skip this section until next year at tax time, don't do it! The sooner you understand what will be needed to complete next year's 1040 form...

...the sooner you can begin organizing your thinking and record keeping to make things much easier on yourself. Also, you can avoid making a costly year-end investment that will unnecessarily raise your taxes (see common misconceptions 1 and 2 which follow).

I promise to do my best at making this as clear as possible—but nobody can keep it from being boring! So go for a cup of coffee if need be, and get ready to make some good notes in the margins.

Mutual funds are among the most flexible of all investments from a tax standpoint. That's the good news. Calculating your taxable income, however, is made more complicated by a maze of rules and exceptions to the rules at both the federal and state levels. That's the bad news.

Because tax laws vary so widely from state to state, I can't proceed very far into planning tax strategies; there are just too many possible scenarios. What I will do is give you a basic foundation so that you can read and plan intelligently in relation to your particular tax bracket and state of residence.

The first major point I want to emphasize is that mutual funds are simply conduits through which individuals invest in securities.

In the process of investing, mutual funds incur capital gains and losses and receive dividend and interest income on their investments. From a tax point of view, all of this is done in behalf of their shareholders. *It's as if you owned all the investments outright, and the gains and losses that result are all your personal gains and losses.* There are three ways mutual funds can generate profits in your behalf:

❶ They invest in stocks that pay dividends. The mutual fund collects the dividends and pays them out to you periodically.

❷ They invest in bonds or short-term debt securities that pay interest. They collect the interest and pay it out to you periodically.

❸ They sell one of their investments for more than they paid for it, thereby making a capital gain. They keep track of these gains (and offset them against any capital losses), and pay them out to you periodically, usually annually. If they end up with more capital losses than gains, they carry the losses over to the next year; you would receive no payment for the year just ending.

All of these payments to you, regardless of the source—whether dividends, interest, or capital gains—are called "distributions." The fund decides whether to make these periodic distribution payments monthly, quarterly, semi-annually, or annually.

A fund goes through a two-step process in making distributions. First, it "declares" the amount of the distribution...

...it intends to make, and sets aside the appropriate amount of cash that will be needed to write you a check. Let's say your fund declares a 25¢ per share distribution, and that there are one million shares owned by investors. This means the fund will be paying out a total of $250,000 to its shareholders at this time. Once the money is earmarked for distribution in this way, the fund no longer counts the $250,000 when it does its daily bookkeeping (see page 10). This has the effect of suddenly lowering the net asset value of the fund—one day the money was being counted as part of the fund, and the next day, the day of the declaration, it wasn't. To indicate to investors that the net asset value is lower than it otherwise would be because of the distribution, an "x" appears next to the name of the fund in the daily newspaper listings (see page 33). The date this happens is called the "ex-dividend" date, *and is the significant date as far as your taxes are concerned.*

The second step of the distribution process is when the fund actually mails your check to you. It can be anywhere from a few days to a month later. This is called the "payment date" and is important only to you (and the other shareholders) because that's when you finally receive the cash that's been promised. The payment date has no significance when computing your taxable income. Let's look at some of the common misconceptions that investors have about fund taxation.

Misconception #1: "It's a good idea to invest in a mutual fund just before one of its periodic distributions."

Actually, it's a bad idea because it will create an immediate tax liability for you. There is no actual profit in owning a fund on the day it goes ex-dividend because the amount the shareholders are to receive is deducted from the value of the fund that same day (see note, below left). If an investor buys a fund today and the fund declares a distribution tomorrow, *the investor owes tax on the amount of the distribution.* This may seem

> ### HOW DISTRIBUTIONS ARE REPORTED IN THE NEWSPAPER
>
> Monday's closing price for the XYZ Fund was $6.00 per share, up 4¢ from Friday's closing price. On Tuesday, the net asset value fell 10¢ a share due to a slight drop in the stock market that day. The fund also declared a 60¢ per share distribution on Wednesday. The listing for XYZ in the newspaper for those two days would look like this:
>
> | | | | |
> |---|---|---|---|
> | Monday | XYZ Fund | 6.00 | + .04 |
> | Tuesday | XYZ Fund | x5.30 | - .70 |

unfair, as the profits were earned by the fund long before the new investor made his purchase. Still, someone has to pay the tax on those profits, and it falls to the "shareholders of record" *at the time of the distribution* to do so.

When a fund makes a distribution, the price of its shares falls by the exact amount of the distribution. This has the effect of reducing the investor's capital gains tax liability in the future. Most funds make distributions at roughly the same time each year, and most funds announce distributions in advance. This presents an opportunity for savings. Just before purchasing shares of any mutual fund, call the fund and ask if a distribution will be made soon. If a distribution is scheduled within a few days, you might want to wait and purchase your shares the day after the distribution to avoid its tax impact.

Misconception #2: "If I don't receive my distribution check until after the end of the year, I don't have to pay taxes on it this year."

From a tax standpoint, distributions fall into two classifications: (1) "capital gain" as described above, and (2) "income," a mutual fund's dividend and interest earnings, less its management fees and other operating expenses. Short and long-term capital gains, interest, and dividend income distributions are all currently being taxed at identical rates.

Your tax liability is based on the ex-dividend date, not the payment date. If the ex-dividend date falls in the current year, your tax liability will also. The fund is required to pre-pare IRS Form 1099-DIV (similar to the one you receive from your employer) for everyone who was a shareholder on any day a distribution was declared. You will receive a copy (and so will the government), which lists the various distributions you will be taxed on, and where to report them on your form 1040 return.

Misconception #3: "As long as I don't sell any of my mutual fund shares, I can't have any capital gains."

This seems logical. Assume you buy fund shares at $10 and still own them at the end of the year. Since it is too soon to know whether you will receive more or less than $10 per share when you sell them, it would seem to follow that it is also too soon to know whether you'll have a capital gain to pay taxes on. What this overlooks is that the mutual fund *itself*, within its portfolio, is continually buying and selling securities. Each time it sells one, it has another capital gain or loss. Since the tax law considers all of this is being done in your behalf, you participate in your fair share of that gain or loss *whenever a fund declares a capital gain distribution*.

When you eventually do redeem (sell) your fund shares, any capital gain or loss from the original purchase must be reported on Schedule D of your form 1040 tax return just like any other investment. One easy way to put off paying this kind of capital gains tax is simply to avoid selling mutual funds for gain just before the end of the year. If you sell in December, then taxes will have to be paid by April 15, just three and a half months later. Instead, you might wait to sell out of a profitable position until the first week of January. The tax on such gains would then not be owed until April of the following year. This postpones paying your tax liability more than 15 months. By the same token, a good time to sell a fund if you have a loss is in December, as the loss will be deductible on the tax return filed only a few months later.

Misconception #4: "To calculate my capital gain from selling my fund shares, I subtract the amount I paid for them from the proceeds I received when selling them."

This is only true in the simplest instance—where you bought all your shares at the same time, received no distributions while you owned them, and sold them all at the same time. In that case, it's pretty straightforward as described. However, if you either receive distributions, acquire your shares over time (for example, through dollar-cost-averaging or reinvesting your dividends), or sell only part of your holdings, there is more work to be done. Let's look at the most common situations.

● **When you receive a distribution.** Keep in mind: *you aren't really gaining anything when you receive a distribution because the amount of the distribution is deducted from the value of your shares.* For example, assume you buy 100 fund shares at $8.00 each. Your total cost is $800. The value grows to $12.00 per share, and your investment becomes worth $1,200 (100 shares multiplied by $12.00 each). If a $1.00 per share dividend distribution is declared, you will receive a check for $100 (100 shares multiplied by $1.00). However, on the ex-dividend date, the value of your shares immediately drops to $11.00 each *because $1.00 per share has been taken out of the fund's asset pool to be mailed to shareholders.* You haven't gained; you still have $1,200 in value—$1,100 in fund shares (100 shares multiplied by $11.00) and $100 cash. (The fund has merely "robbed Peter to pay Paul.")

The tax consequences work like this. If you had sold your shares *before* the ex-dividend date, you would have a $400 capital gain ($1,200 proceeds minus $800 cost). If you sell your shares *after* the ex-dividend date, you would have a $300 capital gain ($1,100 proceeds minus $800 cost) *plus* $100 in dividend income; thus, you still have total taxable income of $400. The ex-dividend date didn't change the amount of your profit; it only changed the tax nature of your profit.

● **When you reinvest your dividends.** If you routinely have your fund distributions reinvested in more shares, you must be careful to avoid double taxation. This is done by adding the cost of the additional shares so purchased to the amount originally invested in the fund when calculating your tax liability. For example, let's take our previous example and make a change: Instead of receiving the $100 distribution in cash,

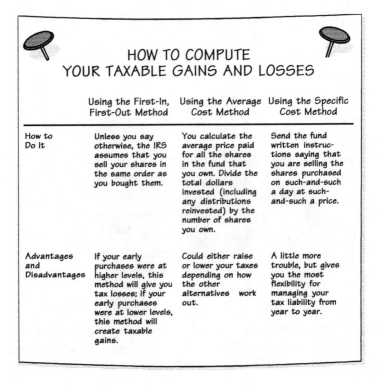

HOW TO COMPUTE
YOUR TAXABLE GAINS AND LOSSES

	Using the First-In, First-Out Method	Using the Average Cost Method	Using the Specific Cost Method
How to Do It	Unless you say otherwise, the IRS assumes that you sell your shares in the same order as you bought them.	You calculate the average price paid for all the shares in the fund that you own. Divide the total dollars invested (including any distributions reinvested) by the number of shares you own.	Send the fund written instructions saying that you are selling the shares purchased on such-and-such a day at such-and-such a price.
Advantages and Disadvantages	If your early purchases were at higher levels, this method will give you tax losses; if your early purchases were at lower levels, this method will create taxable gains.	Could either raise or lower your taxes depending on how the other alternatives work out.	A little more trouble, but gives you the most flexibility for managing your tax liability from year to year.

you instruct your fund to re-invest it in more shares. On the ex-dividend date, the value of the fund dropped to $11.00 per share. At that price, the $100 would purchase an additional 9.09 shares, bringing your total shares to 109.09. The $100 distribution must be reported on that year's federal 1040, and taxes must be paid. Later, you sell all of your shares for $11.00 each, which brings in proceeds of $1,200 (109.09 shares multiplied by $11.00 per share). Will you be taxed on your $400 gain? No. The total cost of the shares (for capital gains purposes) is the initial $800 *plus the $100 on which tax has already been paid,* making a total of $900. Thus, the taxable capital gain from the $1,200 proceeds received the following year is only $300 rather than $400.

● **When you dollar-cost-average.** If you routinely add to your fund holdings through frequent new purchases, you should be especially careful to keep careful records of the dates, amounts invested, and number of shares purchased. That's because you will later need detailed and accurate information concerning your many different purchases in order to compute any capital gains that might result when your shares are eventually sold. This is all the more true if you later sell part (rather than all) of your shares. See the chart below for an explanation of the choices you have under the tax laws. Once you select one of these methods for a particular fund, you must use it every time you sell shares from that fund.

Under the general heading of "other assorted things you should know" are the following items.

● The IRS is available year round to answer your tax questions—call 1-800-829-1040. It also offers free materials on various topics—call 1-800-829-3676 to request IRS forms and publications. You can begin with publication 910, which is an explanation of all the *other* publications they have available.

● The best tax advantage available for mutual fund investing is to carry out as much of your long-term program as possible within an IRA or other tax-deferred type of account.

● Whenever you "switch" between funds at the same organization, it's the same as selling your shares in the fund you are leaving. Unless you are moving out of a money market fund, every switch has tax consequences.

● Using the special checks your fund supplies also has tax consequences (except for money market funds). That's because the fund sells some of your shares in order to honor your check. This is more likely to happen with investors who are using a short-term bond fund in place of a money market fund.

● Investors in tax-free funds don't completely avoid dealing with tax considerations. For example, capital gains distributions from the funds and capital gains you might make on the sale of your shares are taxable just like with any other security. Tax-free income is generally free from federal tax, but not all the dividends you receive will necessarily be exempt from state tax; check with your fund to be sure. Special rules apply under a variety of situations (for example, if you receive income from shares in a tax-free bond fund held for six months or less and sold for a loss). Request IRS Publication 564 for more information on the taxation of mutual funds.

● If you invest in international stock and bond funds, mutual funds are to notify you if you are entitled to claim a tax credit or deduction for taxes *that the fund paid to a foreign country.* For more information, request IRS Publication 514.

● Information you will receive from your mutual fund includes: statements telling you the date, price, and number of shares transacted when buying and selling fund shares; form 1099-B reports the proceeds from selling shares during the year which you can use to help you compute your capital gains or losses; and form 1099-DIV reports the details of dividend and capital gain distributions for which you owe taxes.

My recommendation is that you not buy or sell *primarily* for tax reasons.

Although I acknowledge that it is legitimate to minimize one's tax liability by using any of the applicable strategies mentioned here, a preoccupation with taxes can be counterproductive. Sometimes a few days can make a big difference as to the price you pay or receive for your shares. Don't let tax considerations sidetrack you from following the disciplines you will be building into your long-term strategy. ◆

Glossary

12b-1 Fees

are daily fees charged to shareholders to help offset the fund's promotional and distribution expenses. Every mutual fund is free to either charge them or not charge them. If they do charge them, they must say so in the prospectus. By regulation, they can be no higher than 1.25% per year.

Asking Price

reflects the sales mark up on a "load" fund. It appears to the right of the net asset value, and indicates the price at which shares in the fund were sold that day. It is usually 5%-8½% higher than the net asset value of the shares because of the commission to the salesperson.

Blue Chip Stocks

are shares of large, well-known companies that have long records of profit growth, dividend payments, and reputations for quality products or services.

Capital Gains

are the profits you make when you sell your investment for more than you paid for it.

Closing Price

is the price at which a security last traded before the close of business on a given day.

Dividends

are payments to shareholders as their share of the profits. They are usually made quarterly and are taxable in the year they are received.

Equity Funds

are mutual funds that primarily invest in stocks.

Fixed Income Funds

are mutual funds that primarily invest in bonds.

Hybrid Funds

are mutual funds that have characteristics of both equity and fixed-income funds.

Investment Company

is the technical name for a mutual fund.

IRA Rollover

is when you take a lump sum payment from an employer's pension plan (because of your retirement or termination of employment) and deposit it into an IRA investment plan account within 60 days. Your current IRAs may also be transferred this way. The IRA rollover can be opened at a bank, S&L, mutual fund or brokerage house and the money then invested in stocks, bonds, or money market securities.

Through an IRA rollover, the capital continues to accumulate tax-deferred until it's withdrawn.

Load Fund
is a mutual fund that is sold to investors through a sales network, typically by stock brokers, financial planners, and insurance agents, and for which the investor pays a markup or sales charge.

Mutual Fund
is a company that combines the funds of many investors into one larger pool of money, and invests the pool in stocks, bonds, and other securities consistent with its area of specialization. For this service, the company typically charges an annualized management fee that approximates 1% of the value of the investment.

Net Asset Value
is the market value of a single mutual fund share. It appears in the newspaper listings under the "bid" heading, which means the fund was willing to bid that amount to repurchase any shares that its investors wanted to sell.

No-Load Fund
is a mutual fund that is sold without a sales markup. This is usually done by the mutual fund organization not using a

sales network and selling directly to the investor. However, be careful. There are some funds that still charge a sales load although they are selling directly to the public.

Open-End versus Closed-End Funds
Open-end funds sell as many shares as necessary to satisfy investor interest. They are the most common kind. Closed-end funds have only a limited number of shares available. To invest, you purchase shares through a stockbroker from other investors who wish to sell theirs.

Portfolio
is a collection of securities held for investment.

Prospectus
is a formal written offer to sell a security. Mutual funds provide them free to investors. They explain the fund's investment objectives, performance history, the fees they will charge, the special services they offer, and a financial statement.

Risk Category
is a way of classifying mutual funds that groups together those with similar investment strategies and similar possibilities of profit and loss. Useful for comparing "apples with apples" when measuring mutual fund performance. There is no "official" list of categories used consistently throughout

the industry. The mutual fund trade association, Morningstar, and Lipper are the three most influential authorities on mutual funds, and they each have their own different (albeit similar) ways to classify funds. Because of the great diversity of funds, their systems have grown to include as many as thirty different categories.

Security
is a financial instrument that is bought and sold by the investing public. The majority are stocks, bonds, mutual funds, options, and ownership participations in limited partnerships. All publicly traded securities are subject to the regulation of the Securities & Exchange Commission.

Securities & Exchange Commission (SEC)
is an agency in Washington that regulates the securities industry. SEC rules govern the way investments are sold, the brokerage firms who sell them, what can be charged for selling them, what information must be disclosed to investors before they invest, and much more. The SEC is charged with looking after the general welfare of the investing public. All mutual funds come under SEC supervision.

Volatility
refers to the tendency of securities to rise or fall sharply in price within a relatively short period of time.

Sound Mind Investing

THE FINANCIAL JOURNAL FOR TODAY'S CHRISTIAN FAMILY

Dear Valued Reader:

I hope this booklet has been helpful to you. If so, I believe you'd enjoy reading through a complimentary issue of my monthly *Sound Mind Investing* financial newsletter. It's based on bibli-cally-based values and priorities (see pages 4-5), and gives you:

Help in setting and achieving realistic, personalized goals. You'll find no claims that I can predict coming economic events or market turns. Mine is a get-rich-slow, conservative strategy that emphasizes controlling your risk according to your age, goals, and personal investing temperament.

Very specific, timely advice. I recommend specific no-load mu-tual funds. For each of four different risk categories, I not only tell you what *what to buy* and *how much to buy*, but just as impor-tantly, *when to sell and buy something else*!

Monthly "economic earthquake" updates. I include an economic primer that will help you understand the implications of the un-folding economic tremors. Plus, there are data and graphs of various economic indicators that will be especially helpful in giving us fair warning if a crisis seems to be approaching.

I'd like you to have the opportunity to see these benefits for yourself. Send in the attached postage-paid card for your free issue—there's absolutely no obligation to subscribe. I hope to hear from you soon!